CHERRY TOMATOES
or
THE MIGHTY TOOTHACHE

Chloe Frances

ISBN 978-1-6961-0289-6

For Guinevere and Beatrix,
and for Avery and Christian.
Thank you for believing in me.

ABOVE THE EARTH

Above the earth, I remember
cradling you in my hot stomach,
toes curled with the rest of my body,
as you laid in my lap.

Above the earth, I
watched you peel the skin off your teeth
and waited for you
to hand it over.

Above the earth, I ate and drank you,
sang to and thanked you,
for putting me on ice,
and reattaching me at the hospital.

Yes, it is here,
above the earth,
that I am turning over,
somersaulting gracelessly overhead,
making myself sick,
all for the chance,
to get caught on you
again.

DINNER IN THE POOL

Dinner is in
the pool tonight.
Later you would sleep on the floor.
—and the look on your face!
as you crawled from the bottom up
the next morning....

The big man eating chicken; once you were
so loud,
but I couldn't feel a spine in your body
when I was holding you up—
you were a wet piece of paper
clinging to skin.

Dinner was in
the pool that night,
face-down in the chlorine
with the rest of my summer.

POOLED ON THE CORNER

And on the way to the train,
I say thank god he didn't move into that house,
now sectioned off with caution tape in the middle of the day,
the winter sun screaming down on the weathered, dirty po-
        lice van and
a black plastic baby carrier-carseat
planted in an idle patch of sludge
pooled on the corner.
I say thank god he didn't love me too much or else I might be
looking down from the second story window,
watching that carseat rock in the wind
instead of feeling it on my face like this.

Then I cross the street,
and shake my head.
It is such a shame,
I think,
that even now,
you tease me with the intangible.

OTHER FOOT

Maybe it's me who wanted to feel big and pretty!

No time was wasted taking the bag off my shoulder—
       I was proud of myself.
So, what? I took a bite out of something bigger
to reclaim what had happened once before,
       this time with a colder stomach,
       and a taller face,
       and no reason to wonder if I should be embarrassed.

Earlier I heard you laugh.
I heard you laugh!
I didn't think I was that kind of person anymore,
       but as I watched you smile
       from across the table
I remembered who I thought I would be by now.

In the hours spent alone
walking home in wrinkled clothes,
I felt the other shoe fall right behind me.

NO. 4

I can tell exactly what you're thinking!
The whole world has burst open;
and it is screaming in your ears
after your nice fourth birthday party....

As the room starts spinning,
you touch my arm and smile;
God comes down from heaven for a night
just to shake my hand.
I say, *"I think I've heard this song before,"*
waiting to be seated in a restaurant with my parents at
          ten years old;
we had driven on the freeway for forty-five minutes
and the winter had killed all the plants.

When we get home, I am the one to unlock the door
and kick the snow off my boots in the front room first.
You follow me into the kitchen without saying anything.
I know you love me the most.

TWO-HANDED

...and that is when I had a turn of my luck;
with the hand that had struck me,
he was lifting me up.
The hand that had fed me,
the hand that still feeds,
the hand pulling strings somewhere inside me....

I was biting the nails
while he was pitting his wits;
I grew too big for his arms and he had one last fit.
I am shining and stubborn, of excellent mind,
and that man with the hands,
he was wasting my time!

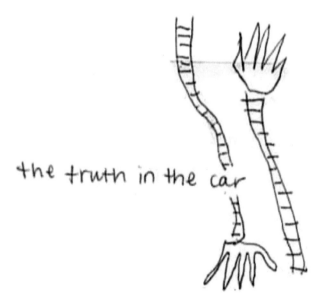

the truth in the car

EMBRYONIC SYMPHONY ORCHESTRA

I wake in a catatonic state
each morning
as the sun starts to pool behind my closed blinds.
The cars and trains and people of the city surrounding my bed
make noise, clamoring and white,
like blood rushing through the body of a mother
while I am curled in the womb;
an embryonic symphony orchestra.

I am waiting, waiting
to be big enough to get out of this room,
this womb,
this hot-pulsing tomb; I am
waiting to be big enough
to walk outside on my own again,
in the sun, where God can see me.

And I am waiting to be pretty again,
so when my mother sees my face
she remembers why she loved me,
and so when I am using my own two legs
to cross the street by your house,
you feel each step shake your windows.

I have deteriorated in this shell,
this hell,
this bomb-shelter belly,
this white-blanket prison cell
long enough.
I am pitiful and quiet and skinny and losing.

I start kicking.

ROTTEN PEACHES/BETWEEN YOUR TEETH

I think of how beautiful it feels,
how I should be so gracious
to rot and sting,
because so many others
don't even have the privilege of being bitten into
to begin with.

I remind myself that it is better to be
moldy and decomposed,
used, bruised, plucked and peeled,
chosen and discarded,
by heavy fist,
than to sit at the top of the tree
waiting for someone
with long-enough arms
or a long-enough neck
to take me down.

To be chewed and spit,
or swallowed and shit–
O, how lucky I should feel
to have been bitten into at all!

IN THE BEGINNING OF IT

When the back of my throat caught fire
and my eyes burned up, I knew
it would not be too long
until my head burst into flames,
and he would watch me act like a child again.

Of course I am embarrassed,
but the heat,
sometimes,
is too strong to keep swallowing,
especially in my condition.

Regardless,
he persists to push
his body to mine,
making sounds that remind me
of my brief time
in the womb—
and it works!

I have melted onto his t-shirt
yet again.

COMING OF AGE IN THE BATHROOM MIRROR

I looked in the mirror
and peeled back the skin of my cheek,
where bruised chalk teeth tumbled over each other like
       rotten fruit,
or rocks that had been worn too thin.

Smacking porcelain gums, I
felt my skin grow paler and looser, I
watched my face melt and mold.
"Soon my head will make my body its box-eared bitch," I thought.
       "...locking herself in the bathroom,
        calling her mother on the phone...."
I guess I thought I was more careful than that.
But as I stood there, scrutinizing that slack-jawed bastard
       in the glass,
I realized I recognized the face
from the toilet bowl water two nights before.

SALT

I was unsure of how to apologize to myself
for not being as tough as I thought I was,
for not being as big or as loud or as smart,
and for not knowing
I was making a mistake
when I crawled in that bed
and dreamt of nothing.

GUTTURAL

There is love in my belly,
big enough for three people;
love, hot in my stomach,
and it's churning around,
getting everything wet with it,
sticky—.
There is love in my belly,
meant for someone else,
leftover,
and over,
turning there, waiting
to be given away—.
There is love in my belly,
and it is so ripe it hurts,
past due, it's rotting—
this love in my belly
was not made for you,
and it will not fill you up the way that it should but
this love in my belly
it has got to come out,
and if I can't give it to her,
I'll have to give it to you.

LAST SUMMER IN WHALON

I closed my eyes and spit
my feminine body into the lake.
The fish, they swam right past it.

I waited for the earth to split—
for the ground beneath my feet to take
me under, let the blue consume my stiff.

When the horsefly under hot sun bit,
I felt the eyes of people set to make
a fool of me with every word I let go limp.

I wish I hadn't left my soul and grit
in that body in the bay,
between the teeth and tongue and ribs and wrist.

But now I'm doomed for shakes and fits,
for dreamless nights and quiet aches,
for lifetimes where it's easier to quit.

I'm left to eat at my own wit,
to watch my body mold and fray,
hoping just to catch a glimpse
of what, to you, I can't admit.

ELEMENTARY

Despite all the difference,
I remain on the losing end,
watching the youth that he loves me for
condemn me to naïvity
that loudly strangles away
any chance I had
of growing up inside of him.

BENTON & WASHINGTON

When my bright and shiny new doctor asked how I felt,
I wanted to tell her
that her house looked like a tall boy,
a real Michael Cera-type,
but with a worse haircut,
more sickly and sad,
like something *Morrissey* would cough up.
He was crooked—always—
kind of leaned to the left—
and when he cried,
the bastard's nose wouldn't stop running.

And there he is!
Standing on the corner of Benton and Washington!
Probably freaking traffic out with his overflowing self-pity,
and I know if I went to school with him,
I would not have been that poor fool's friend.

But instead I told her I felt fine,
and asked her how her day was going, because,
let's be honest,
it was a pretty dumb thought to have.

CHRISTENED

His hands were cold but so was I,
so rudely awakened by the reality
of what I thought I wanted.

I sat in his bathroom,
disillusioned for the last time.
I was trying to turn the stones in my stomach
into a victory.
Then I walked back into his bedroom and was victorious
      again and again,
        silently,
until I asked him to please take me home
the next day.

I left teeth under his pillow
and kissed him goodbye,
and afterward, I showered for a long time
trying to flush him out.
I wonder if I am still under his fingernails,
and if he is proud of himself
for feeling like a boy again.

I have been Christened.

COMPANY

All of my family surrounds me to watch
as the big, bad, and arrogant gets knocked down a notch.
I have all the company in the world for this magnificently tragic
show; it is
me on the surface and empty below; *oh!,*
how I saw this coming!, how I saw this coming!!

You didn't believe me then, and you won't hear it from me now, but
a year before I met you, I had figured you out.
I was hot-gleaming, steaming, dirty wheels on the van—
I drove it to the lake and I didn't look back. I sat
watching water for months.

Now, again, I am entranced,
but by a much greater body,
this time
free of the ignorance.

RECONSTRUCTION

He took a sledgehammer
to my knees,
and watched me wince in pain.

I smiled slightly then,
because he did not know
that I had already taken
that sledgehammer
to my own knees,
and breasts,
stomach, teeth, and tongue;

he did not know
that I had already seen
jaws like his before
in the mirror
and the water,
baptizing myself
for the eighteenth time;

and he did not know
that I loved him
because it felt clean and right
to be seen
as I saw myself—

someone who deserves a sledgehammer to their
kneecaps
and spit in their eyes!

"NICE HAIR"

I know you've felt it before,
when your mother comes down the stairs
it's in your tummy.

Like a man, he speaks to you,
like a dog, he sees through you…
"You should figure out beforehand
which one of you
is going to get to be the child."

I'm leaving and you're watching from
the second story window.
I turn to look and you're not there,
but I still feel you watching me.
Oh, how lovely my adult body has become,
won't you watch it for a couple minutes more?
Something bastard in my chest
when you closed your eyes.

On the way home I notice how slowly the snow is falling like
feathers from *ten thousand dead doves!*
And I think to myself it is too bad I didn't see this pretty peaceful
        drift before,
when I was
face-down in the pavement of the alley next door,
empty-stomach heaving up
my proximity to you.

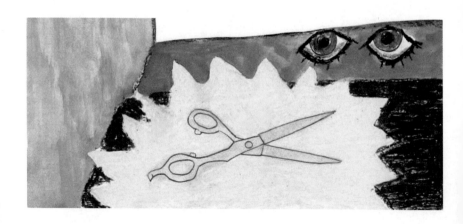

26

28

29

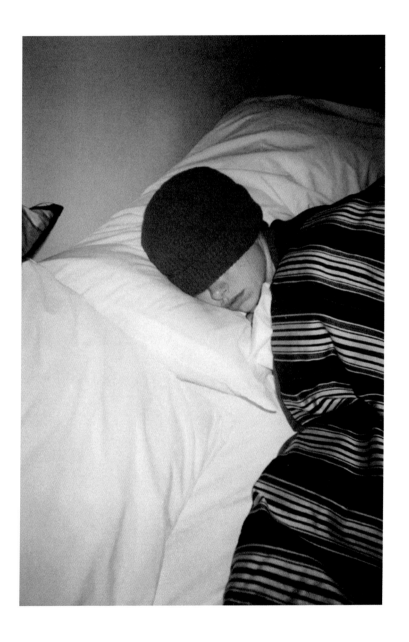

UNDERNEATH THE SOUTH
THERE IS DIRT

Telephone wire buzzing hot
     in the backyard.
The kids play badminton right over its head
while cotton floats down o'er fields in warm rain.
And the trees standing guard
as young boys shoot the squirrels.
Like teeth, baring pride on prepubescent shoulders;
emulating some version of men, cowboys, and fathers—
For a second, I envy their primitive naïvety.
The melancholy on my back?,
their hoses and sprinklers take care of that.
Their trucks go to town and their trucks go to church,
mothers smoke over dinners,
the men go to work.
I'm driving down south, away from that city,
away from the sounds and the lights and the pity,
watching Alabama babies spit chlorine in the pools.

It hasn't dawned on them yet,
and I don't think it ever will.

ANGEL

It had been a long time since I prayed
or called my mother
or felt good enough to walk from my bedroom to the kitchen.

But at least I got to see your face
when I walked in with that big, shiny ribbon pinned to my chest,
so clean and pristine.
'I am doing so great,' I smiled to you.
'I am the greatest in the world.'
Then I sank to your level for the second time that morning
and watched you shut down in the opposite direction.
It came full circle,
almost,
as I shrouded your back,
this time without touching you.

OSTRICH

On Thursdays,
after the yellow house,
I return to the "taken-for-granted" blue.

In between, however,
I do not hesitate to watch myself
grow into the person I spat on at nine....

"How did that baby get so old?"

—and as I turn to close the door,
she looks me in the face and asks me
if I like what I have become.
I didn't have the heart to tell her

that on Thursdays after school,
I walk through town to a gloom-yellow house,
and pray to a woman who gets paid just to grin at me,
because after all this time,
I'm still too ashamed to turn to God for any help.

Instead,
I kiss her on the forehead,
shut the door behind me, and
as soon as the breeze hit my face,
I take my head off my shoulders
and bury it two feet
underground.

"WOMAN"

I am now an adult
in the body I bore as a child.
I cannot see where that body ended
and this one began,
but I have been told that that life is over,
over and over again.
I guess the others
can see something different,
can smell something on me,
they tell me I am, "womanly."

But I feel him ache, that child inside of me,
that I have wrapped up in layers
of experience
and loss of innocence.
To pull them off would be
to return to naïvety;
to be without the memories
of the forbearing things that have maimed me.

As I get older and no taller, I worry
that I am losing the face that keeps me easy to forgive.
Arduously, I protect
any pretty things that I have left,
and I wait, for I know I will give them up, anyway;
I have always loved the adrenaline in being unfortified,
and to be desired, admired, adored and acquired?
is to be loved!

13 WAYS OF LOOKING AT HEAVEN

*Inspired by Wallace Stevens's "13 Ways of Looking at a
Blackbird"*

I

In dreams I softly kiss you,
and through faded memory,
I cut myself
on the edge of Heaven.

II

Eaten alive by
sharp teeth, maggot and fly,
to rise like pools of heat
and eat away at Heaven's gate.

III

Through the stereo,
David sings slowly of Heaven,
and I get a shiver
down my brand-new spine.

IV

The summer those peaches
in your backyard swelled with flesh,
Heaven dripped down my chin
and into the pool.

V

In the corner of my eye,
and at the end of the bed,
I caught Heaven
lingering
just long enough
to make out the ribs
of a dirty, leaden angel.

VI

Numb with glee, I took Heaven to my knee,
and shattered it softly and cleanly.
Thanked it for waiting eighteen years all for nothing,
and kissed it goodbye very sweetly.

VII

Heaven was held against me,
but now my arms are long enough
to cast it away
and forget about its glory.

VIII

We were burned alive by bared-tooth grins
and ashes in the backseat.
Yes,
Heaven was not too far
tonight.

IX

On Wednesday,
Heaven reached down
its long, scaly fingers
and picked away
at the dead skin
on my hands.

X

As an ugly virgin takes her last breath,
what was warm becomes vapid,
and what was known as Heaven
becomes something foggy
someone wishes they could remember
the colors of.

XI

In ruby red shoes and red gingham sundress,
I try to accept
that this walk down the street
is the closest I will ever get
to Heaven.

XII

Two stories above
the room that you relish,
Heaven pulls on my strings,
and you follow with settled heart.

XIII

Heaven has gnawed its way
through my stomach
for the last
and most beautiful time.

BIRTHDAY CAKE

My stomach did the trapeze
as I stepped out on the porch,
you were trying very hard not to look at me.
I smoked my whole cigarette,
all in two-drags-and-one-breath,
and left before the birthday cake was served.

Baklava for breakfast
and I'm waiting for the train.
You have a hundred years of love in you
and still you fear the name!

This monkey on my back is turning black,
a cancerous tumor;
thought I could get through to her
with my sense of humor.

I never understood your smoker's cough until it
        became mine,
and when I close my eyes
I see your lungs collapsing one more time;
by the lake where I had slept,
I watched you gasp until you wept;
saw something kind of ugly in you then,
and that is when
I made up my mind.

TO GO TO CHURCH AGAIN

He's a slick southern star,
I'm his mean little junkie.
He comes up from the west,
so he can smoke up and fuck me.
His cologne stains my clothes
so he lingers when he's leaving.
My cherry red toes
match my brackish heart beating.

He's a smooth Texan charmer
with a glint in his teeth.
You can tell from his grin
that his passion is sweet.
When lays his rough hands
on my unsullied body,
I dream of all things
still holy and rotten.

UH-OH!

Eventually,
she covers herself
in enough beads and lace
to look like some
caricature of my maternal grandmother.

She grins at me, all her teeth coming loose,
what a bull in a china shop
this pink-pussied doll is!
What a mockery of a storm,
of a Midwestern tornado siren
blowing through the TVs to the basement.

I dress her up and bend her arms
and the men, they all adore her.
But when her brother comes to town—

WICKER PARK FOUNTAIN (EMPTY)

melted ice cream

i watched you brush your teeth
and spit blood in the sink
    i was not homesick at all
in fact,
i could feel the blood in my hands and feet
and when you put your hands on the front door
    the gate
    the garage door
    the tile beside the pool
i counted my teeth.
i could not believe
i was a child again.

basketball

They banged on the window at noon
and i watched your head move
    slowly at first
then all at once, you gripped the side of your bed
    rolled off
    and closed the curtain.
in the dark i could still see your red hair.

POINTER FINGER (I AM THE BIRD)

I was struck with God's fist,
I was cursed with the mark!
I was damned from the get,
I was doomed from the start!
Soon all thats left
will be bones and the meat,
I will show it around,
it will look just like me—!

Throughout your vengeance,
I sought mercy from worms,
but I am the bird! I am the bird!

PIQUA

Nine or ten years old,
some funeral home in Ohio,
his daughter is crying;
I kiss his cold forehead.
The powdery makeup
meant to make him look living
sticks to my lips
like flour or sand.
It is then that I start
my ten-year game of martyr
cause I'm my mother's daughter
and her mother before her.

My cousin and I
get lice from the coat racks,
some kid with a dead aunt—*or was it the helmets?*—
still we both laugh.

DUCKLING

You are not an angel, you are a pet.
I look at you through glossy eyes;
I'm sorry I haven't let you go yet.

We're plucking the last of our feathers out
one by one;
in this second I am
squished fingers in a
desperate touch.

I want to say something about your posture,
about how I noticed its sudden shift
and how I know that you are anxious.
The way you are sitting reminds me of the night at your place
when
I got too high and sloppily told you I needed you.
Instead, I
say nothing because
I know I'd rather not hear the answer.
Instead, I
sink back into the couch.

I wonder what you are thinking.
I never find out.

PERSISTENCE IN AGONY

On broken leather taxi seat, on airline carpet,
and on the edge of warm pool tile, I loved you.
In moving warehouse, in dampened home,
and in foreign arms, I loved you.
Through drooping skull, through ceramic bowls,
through cut t-shirts and pants, I loved you.
And from under wing with quiet persistence,
I love you.

PERSON ON ~~TRAIN~~ IN FRONT OF US.
BUS

23W370

In the morning the field would pool with mist,
and my stomach would hang below my knees.
I held her body as she clung to her pride;
I was carrying something much bigger than me.

In the afternoons, the grass would be dry,
and the trees would grow arms of their own.
I was a coward then, I just didnt know yet.
I will always dream of that home.

On holiday, still, when I bound down those stairs,
the floor sings of the things that it's done;
pinned up and proud is the heart of that woman
in the crest on the wall with the velvet of blood.

Eenie-meanie, tipsy-teenie,
apple jack John.
Sweetchie-ochie-toechie,
dominochi
ee, ta, tiss.

THE SUN

It is hard to remember now,
the days of sleeping in the darkroom during class
and breathing in dust like a trophy in the downtimes.
For the last three months,
it was always quiet—
        certainly—
and it always felt like my head
was floating six feet above my shoulders.

Now I should deluge myself
over evidence of a pulse
when I have finally caught my breath in this life?
Nothing seemed worse to me than
burying the guinea pig in the backyard
between the bushes
in a hand-painted tomb.

Let me keep *that* sorrow here—
let me keep yellow medicine, vaccinations,
        and the wasp between my heel and the doormat.

Yes, I'd rather lose each of my wicked incisors again,
than stand here facing the sun
with my head on a string any longer.

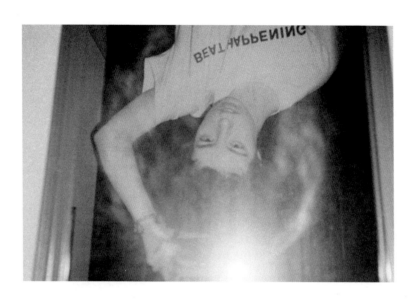

TOOK OUR SHOES OFF
AT THE PARK

THE KIDS AND THEIR
PARENTS MOVED AWAY
FROM US

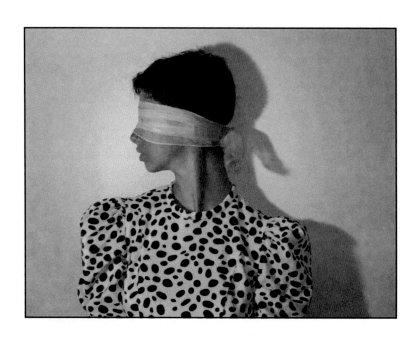

UP AND OUT

Even disconnected
I feel It bite my toes,
push its way up and out,
and digest the thought of me.
In It's sleep It says my name
and I listen to It,
even though I know I will regret it.

By the way—
It has come up a million times since I last saw you,
and your lap was never there
to catch it.

SO THIS IS HOW WE LAY NOW

So this is how we lay now,
like dogs in heat,
bleeding between legs and mouths,
no longer pushing and prodding at loose teeth and swollen flesh;
flat on our stomachs
pooling with warm blood.
Waiting and quiet—
shaved heads,
soft fingernails,
tugging at the dead skin below us,
moving between whispers instead of for them;
broken bones,
rolled eyes and tongues
no longer meeting in flame,
but rather with a momentary disposition,
lost between train tracks and asphalt,
scraped away by jagged fingers.
This is how we lay,
like dead animals being picked apart by vulture and fly,
waiting for something to start again.

PRETTY PINK PURSUIT
of all things, to hate fruit!
The sweetest, like lips,
and their seeds and their pits.
I bury it deep inside of my abdomen,
and watch these things grow from my belly button,
making my gut clean and tough.

Between the teeth rests
salt and street
from sweating for a few
in a cold, crowded basement—
I wonder if you can see on my face what
I felt the night before?
Regardless, I follow your head down through forest and debris
and sigh out in pleasurable boredom.

PATRONAGE

This dance we keep up,
it is making me weak;
this polite say-hello-and-goodbye,
drifting around what we are both trying
to forget,
softly,
but it is still there,
stale in the air.

We are dancing very sweetly
because we still don't want to stop.
It has become such a tired performance,
filled with calculated moves to keep us going,
to keep ourselves in orbit of each other.

This dance we are doing,
it is keeping me weak;
these kind and light steps, they feel heavy and hollow.
My feet have become two gelatin anvils moving independently
of my torso.

Yes, we both wish it was over,
and yet!
neither of us will bow.

UNSEEN, UNDESIRED, INEVITABLE

...and all the while that fist does shake,
and those legs do kick,
and those arms do break;
all tucked away into a cabinet of things
unseen, undesired, and inevitable.
But holy eyes pale in comparison
to those maternal and scrutinizing;
they live inside me,
and when I am not looking,
they are—
yes!
After all these miles those shakes wont quit,
and these teeth dont slacken,
and those mouths still spit,
all waiting to be purged through brutalized skin;
unseen, undesired, and inevitable.

GOD'S FUNNY EYES
in the back of Momma's head.
O, what a blessing
to be that gullible again.

You on the other hand, burning through my fist.
I WAS A CHILD SET ON FIRE, waiting to feel bliss.
Now I walk on skin like needles and bandages,
and dance on wounds in devils' shoes.

One more muscle pulled,
one more thread in the sweater left yet to be unraveled.
Maybe if I didn't wear that suit...
and maybe if you wore bigger boots...
but we are different creatures still..!
BURNING, BRUTAL, ILL

TRIPPING IN MY PLATFORM SHOES
IN FRONT OF THE MIDDLE SCHOOLERS

Down into the street I went,
the sunlight screamed my name,
in front of all the children squealing—
inarguably my most human court yet!—
and with every sharp and pointed exhale
from their familiar crony mouths,
I fell from grace, humbled again....
"This is just what I deserve," I guessed.
My bony ankles speaking tongues,
I trudged on and on and on,
I was young again,
a child's friend,
they were God, they were God, they were God.

TRIPPING IN MY PLATFORM SHOES
IN FRONT OF THE MIDDLE SCHOOLERS *(Alternate Version)*

Down onto the street I went
for every man to see,
eating fucking pavement
at the sweet age of nineteen.
My lipstick on, my hair brushed nice
my pearly whites an eggshell gate,
I spewed those curses, damned my shoes
and the punks all gawked with hate.
Their rough-and-tumble thund'ring rumbles
of laughter left me blue,
but in my gut I felt it churn
and did not condemn them with my hand for I knew—
the face of innocent criticism I met with whirling haste,
and a quiet appreciation
that the tables had not yet been turned,
and that I will not be there to see it
when they finally move in their abiding manner.

GOD IS A SHOWERHEAD IN H********* B****

Often, I am turning towards you;
in these dreams I open quietly.

Often, I am speechless in a heavy crowded room,
bleeding from my gut and mouth,
tugging at coattails and shirt sleeves for help,
but I am told to stop making such
        a big deal out of nothing.

Often, I am left with sweat and tears,
jerking awake violently and too early,
stuck with the unsettling
yet familiar taste
of nickels in my mouth.

But now, out of the bathroom window,
I can hear the words you once so sweetly called me ringing.
I made sure to keep this moment virgin to my imagination.

This is not a dream, no—
this has flesh and blood and scabs to pick.
After you cut the umbilical cord, I taught
myself to walk by watching the girls on TV,
and now I am in your backyard,
packing faith under my kneecaps like soil in a pot,
and binding them up with five-year-old gauze
        from the medicine cabinet.

BRUNCH AT

And there it all is; laid out in front of me like some
Bob Evans buffet after church!
All I have to do is reach out and take what I want.
It feels too easy.

There it all is:
waiting for my grubby little hands,
—or grimy or greedy—
tearing holes in the plastic tablecloth.

There it all is,
so pristine and so precious.
It is all mine!
and I am too scared to touch it.

THE WOMAN OF WHALON HAS SEEN MY FACE

Through the winter with no end,
in my boredom, dreamt of you.
Wondered what I'd have to do;
pondered what it would be like to.
Through some love for you, my friend,
in my lonesome dreamt of you.
Wondered if you could really love me
the way you always say you do.
I am burning at the edges!
Turning into men I've loved before,
and in the meantime finding ways
to settle some younger devil's score.

I sat in the pews
crying off all my colors,
watching the adults move
Easter decorations around.
I was asking very nicely,
in a quite pathetic manner,
to be forgiven, to be forgiven, to be forgiven.
So when we were driving home,
and the lake was just about to close,
I took your hand, and feeling damned, I thought,
"He loved me once and that should be good enough."

Parking
down the street
by the angel's house;
all the trees are taller than me.
They're showing her things
I'm too dumb to see.

Walking
through the field
past the angel's house;
the ground caves beneath my feet.
I'm looking for something
that I'm too dumb too see.

O, all the winter I was nineteen,
I let you be my swollen fantasy.
Swimming in the lake;
I can't see,
I can't see,
I can't see.

RENASCENCE

Our bodies are filled up with devils and junk,
with cats and dogs and bicycles, medicine, and other stuff
that makes us grind our teeth at night,
and walk too fast in the grocery store.

The Tootsie Rolls on the counter looked older than me;
I thought pathetically to myself that if you were here you'd eat
one
anyway.
I shiver through seasons, swim through stages of grief and luck,
and I am simmering on hot at the edge of the pot.

And these days, it smiles at me from around every corner;
it rides in on first light and goes only when I get too cocky.
Every time I wished to be older as a child has come true.

I'm discovering the grace in being a hedonist again.
I was raised not to spit on the sidewalks and I could never marry
someone who did,
but my domestic (or maybe suburban) vision of diplomacy was
        nothing more than that,
and with time, has been gouged and popped and carefully picked
        off.

And beneath it all,
I have been waiting,
because to touch the surface again and again is the fecundity
        I live on,
and the God that made me
gave me hands that can only reach upward.

2 00 BLACK CARAVANS

driving up MY street!
Blocking my driveway—
how awesome for me—
I get to wait
while 200 black caravans
drive and drive and drive,
through my neighborhood.

All in a line,
like a freight train of giant ants
holding up the trip to the cousins'.

200 black caravans.
I do not know where they are going
and I do not care.
I just wish they would hurry up
because I have a Zumba class to be punctual for.

HOPEFUL 1

I think I am not supposed to be in love
in the way that moms and dads are
or in the way that couples who become bands are
or in the way that directors and comedians are.
I do not think I was made for love,
for an equal love;
I do not think I was made for a partner like that,
but I do think that one day
I might have a child
and they will be my greatest love yet
and all the loneliness I have ever felt
will be drowned out and dried up by the face of my baby
and when they sleep on my chest
I will feel the love I have ached for my whole life
fill up my lungs and my stomach
and nothing else will matter. It will be me and this kid
against the world
until this kid grows up and can choose not to love me.
But worry not!
I have been practicing for
non-reciprocating love my whole life!
And by then it will be but a drop
in a very gorgeous, big bucket.
This is not a sad poem,
this is a very hopeful one!
I am not going to be in love the way I always dreamed
because I have a much bigger love on its way to me.
Not a sad poem.
hopeful one

A BIG AERIAL SURPRISE

A race, a loop-de-loop,
a twist and a pull,
parts of the sky falling right into
the backyard pool.
What a silly summer day
for all of this to go down.
I will spend the autumn
fishing out all these pieces,
drain the pool, then
tarp it up.

A big aerial surprise!
Pieces of the sky,
backyard pool.
How silly.
I will spend the autumn
fishing out the pieces.
It seems
it always happens this way!

A BAD MAMMA-JAMMA
pulling up on her hog.
The tires scream,
the asphalt steams,
and the leather reeks of smog.
What a bad mamma-jamma
who has just driven her motorcycle
right into
my front living room window.
I am not even mad
about all of the broken glass,
or the inconvenience this repair will cost me,
because she is so cool,
and badass.
Yeah.
A bad mamma-jamma,
that's what she is,
and she crashed right through,
right into my lap.
Thank you, God,
for this hot, biking angel.
"Mother of my child,
child of my heart,
we must never be apart..."

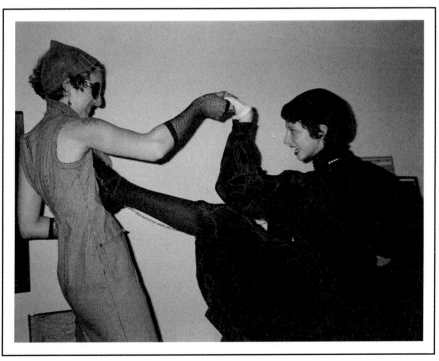

SMALLEST THING (BETTER THAT WAY)

Sunset seeping in through curtain,
I am smaller than everything,
and I'm starting to like it better that way.
I've just woken up to
the sound of the dying-down,
the sound of the going-home,
the end of the day,
and still I have my witching hours left!
To fill with food and ornaments,
to seal away my restless pride,
to retire now to chamber, bedside.

Sunrise peeking in through curtain,
I am smaller than everything,
and I'm starting to like it better that way.
Eyelids sink with weight of cinder,
body sings a heavy song,
hands and heart go soundly under cover;
I'll come to when this new day has gone.

PAVEMENT

When the pavement gets hot
you can peel it off the ground
in dirty, burning chunks
in front of everyone else,
and when the ground gets wet
you can pick up the worms.
Nothing will hurt;
these days are the first.

VS.

ASPHALT

When I was a child,
loose in the summer,
I grieved, but I didn't know why.
Now on these streets,
whose asphalt burned my knees,
I carry you into the night.

PEARL

I paid the price,
pearling and white.

It's like watching TV
and everyone I love is on every channel.
Just like a dream!
Just like a dream!
And I never have to wake up,
and I never have to eat,
and when I look out the window,
the whole world is screaming beneath my balcony.
I dangle my baby
in front of them all;
he never falls.
When I look in the mirror
something gorgeous stares back at me,
bearing its teeth in a gruesome grin,
because it has everything,
everything it could ask for,
and there is nothing left for me to want.
How boring!...

PIANOS AND MATH

I have heard playing piano is like math.
I have never been good at math.
An out-of-tune piano has always lived at my paternal grandmother's house, and I have been in love with it since before I could talk.
Every day I would sit with it and sing with it and play it until I had to leave.
By seven I would hit random keys for hours believing I was making beautiful music. Every year I asked for piano lessons but never got them. So by twelve I would learn songs by ear and continue poking out mutilations of notes and chords.
I learned which ones I liked best by trial and error. I would rarely touch the black keys.
By twenty I would see my grandma nearly 260 days less per year than I would as a child, which happens to be a lot of days. Recently upon one of these rare visits, I found myself wandering to the Yamaha to make cacophonies we both enjoyed. She told me that nobody has touched it since I don't play it anymore.
I left that afternoon and I would not play that piano again.

I have never been good at math, no, but it has never mattered to me.

This is a Preface to an Essay That You Probably Might Skip Over, Maybe, and That is Okay, but I Am Here If You Need Me

The thing you are about to read means a whole stinking lot to me. I wrote it all in one night. I was trying to go to bed and then all of a sudden all these words came barreling into my brain and said, "If you do not write us down right this second well then, by George, you are going to go crazy." And I thought, "It is 1:30 in the morning, I am trying to sleep for cryeye! I will let you out tomorrow." But the words did not listen and just kept coming and then there were too many to ignore. So I started writing and did not stop and did not sleep until the next day at, like, eight in the morning. It all came out in one big flush which is a very unrealistic expectation of the artistic process but I'm just telling you what really happened so don't get your panties in a twist.

This thing you are about to read is a whole big account of every love I have ever had in my life, including but not limited to: romantic partners, expressing myself through performance, and kissing dead bodies. It is the story of a very bad time when I felt not-so-good and actually felt pretty "severely depressed" or whatever my therapist likes to say. But this story is a hopeful one!! It is the story of how I hit rock bottom in my friend's apartment 2,000 miles away from my house and then decided to pull myself up by my bootstraps and start the process of working toward my Good goals instead of wanting to die and whatnot. My friends said it made them cry so I thought maybe I should include it so I can make some of you cry, too. Ha! Enjoy.

89

CRANK

Chloe Frances

I froze my body. Yes! You heard me right. I cryogenically
froze my body. It was my own choice and no one made me do it but I
did it and now here I am, unfrozen years later to tell the tale.

It all started in 2008. Well, really it started the second I was
born, in 1999, very early on a morning smack dab in the middle of sum-
mer. It started right then but it didn't really start then because even
though my blood was pumping and my eyes were open, I hadn't turned
my brain-light on yet.

I turned on my brain-light, which is exactly like what it sounds
like, when I was nine years old. I remember this because before I was
nine I said lots of things that children don't usually say and did lots
of things that an ornery senior would do. I didn't care about anything
except myself because I was still just an animal and not even a good
one. I would step on entire anthills and colonies claiming I was, "break-
ing them," putting to use some great dominance I had over them. I
remember watching my cousin and my grandma cry over movies like
My Girl and *Old Yeller* and thinking that anyone who cries at movies
is dumb and weak like what a shark would think of a seal if that seal
flopped around on the surface of the water and cried during sad mov-
ies. I remember seeing my mom cry when her dad died, and knowing
that I'd never get to talk to him again or see his face or ask him a ques-
tion that I had just thought of and was pretty bummed out but just

thought, "All things die," and I guess in defense of that empty, cold nothingness that used to occupy the body I live in now, I did not know him very well and didn't have a concept of death yet.

I remember being eight years old and going to my great-grandpa's 100th birthday party and being scared to touch him because his skin was so thin I thought if I touched it too hard I might poke a hole right through it and then all of his inside-forearm-gunk would come out like squeezing a rotten plum. It didn't. Then I remember being nine years old and staring down at the dead body of my great-grandpa in a casket with all the same people in the same city we were in just a year before, except this time they were not serving delicious marble-layered cake with buttercream frosting. Instead, everyone was crying in various parts of the tiny, dim room. My cousin didn't want to look at him very long but I was okay with looking at him because he just looked asleep with lots of flour-y makeup on, and it is not everyday that I get to see a real dead body so I might as well utilize the opportunity. The room was dark except for one light over his body and I wonder now if somebody requested it be that way or if the funeral homes always do that. Either way I would like to say, "Thank you," to the person who chose it to be that way because the room has since been a gorgeous staple of some very lonely dreams even when there's not a wake happening inside it. My grandma who I loved very much like a perfect mother or best friend came up to my cousin and I and she was crying very hard and I had seen her cry during *Old Yeller* so I was not very surprised and she asked if one of us could please give him a kiss on the forehead. I looked at my cousin and her eyes got all big, like how people talk about deer in headlights, and without saying a word she told me, "I am not going to do it. The thought of kissing a dead person's body really grosses me out even if it is the father of the mother of my mother, and I'm sorry that by forfeiting this I am forcing it to be you who kisses his forehead but it certainly won't be me." Well, as aforementioned, I was lacking the concept of death, I had no reservations toward it and I wasn't going to say no to my grandma because there was really no reason to and I knew that when people are dead sometimes you have to do important things for the people that knew them. I plunged my forty-pound body over the side of the casket and planted a big smooch on his freckled German forehead and immediately my brain spotlighted the message, "Oh yes! Dead dead bodies are cold; I knew this but forgot until just now!" His makeup stuck to my lips, and I made a note to wipe off my mouth but only after my grandma walked away so she would not think that I was at all inconvenienced by this kiss. She was very pleased with me, and praised me for this small thing which was No-Big-Deal, and migrated to another corner of the room. When she did, my cousin turned to me and said something to the effect of, "Wow! I can't believe you did that. I could not have done that." Later, I told my parents and they were also shocked by my big deed. All of that shock and admiration for doing something bold and brave that other children probably would not felt very good. It was like a new kind of good, like something was bubbling inside of me and the steam was looking for a way out. But nothing was bubbling. No - as it turned out, there was actually a tiny machine the size of a 1940's style flashbulb press film camera pressed up in between my stomach and my heart!

This little machine had a crank and all these nine years this crank had been either budged accidentally or missed entirely. The little machine was a hand-powered generator and for the first time in that Ohio funeral home I had figured out how to crank it all by myself. And when I did this, it sent voltz and zoltz and zaps of electricity up my spinal cord right into the light bulb in my head which had previously been only bursting with light every so often when my parents would crank the handle while I performed for them or when my friends would crank it when we played Witches and Mermaids. Suddenly I started cranking it everyday (not in the masturbation way, in the very innocent self-exploration way, which I guess also sounds like masturbation). I discovered I could make myself very bright with light shooting out of my mouth and nose and ears and the holes where my eyeballs are supposed to be and people loved when I did it. The light made me happy and the light made adults happy and the light made my peers happy. And I could shoot this light out all the time and it would never run out because I was the one cranking the handle and I was always with me to crank my own handle so there was really no lack of manpower in the generator department.

You are probably thinking, "This is very sweet but in the beginning of this story you said something about freezing yourself cryogenically which is a feat not many can pull of and I would like to hear about that now or sometime soon." Well, to you I would say, "Okay!" and also, "Hold your horses!" because I think it is important that you know that I cranked the handle to my own generator all by myself for a very long time and that all through my preteens and teenage years I cranked it so much that the light absolutely never went off and I was a very happy, socially-adept, and successful little lady who knew how to charm and people-please (in a genuine way) and please themselves also.

When I was sixteen, I met a person who was not even supposed to be where he was the day I met him, but came out of happenstance. I think now about how different things would be if this person decided an hour or so was too long to drive on the California highways that day and never came at all. But he did and I am very grateful for it.

When I first met this person, I didn't think anything of him. He was quiet and shy and kept to himself. Then we started talking and I realized very quickly that I didn't want that to stop for as long as I could listen. The first thing I noticed about him was the goddamn size of this man's brain-light generator. I thought, "This thing is so giant! It might be the biggest one I've ever seen!! And it fits right there in his skinny little chest behind all those rib bones?! I can't believe it!" Somehow, an hour or so later, we found ourselves alone even though we were still in this huge convention hall with thousands of bodies and people all around and very close to us. Even though we just met my light made him know that we were the same kind of person and he could tell me important things and I would understand them. He told me about how his generator had not been touched for a few years; he said that it was dusty and that one day he had accidentally gotten distracted with Bad Things that he forgot to crank it and now the muscles in his arms were not strong enough to crank it by himself. He seemed completely unaware that even though he did not think the generator was working, he still had a lot of leftover energy from when it was, and his lightbulb was totally on and the light was coming right out of his face and shining into mine. Even when his generator was off, his light was almost double the brightness of mine. I was jealous but not in a malicious way.

I admired him very much quite immediately and I think that is when I fell in love with him. I like to think that it was a decision - that I said, "Okay, yes, I love this thing," like when someone asks me to try a new food and I have to tell them right then and there after the first bite what I think. But it was not like that at all, not really.

It was more like if you ordered a package of four very special long-lasting batteries and this package did not arrive in two days like it said it was supposed to, and eventually you lose hope that it will ever come, and go on with your life, forgetting about those and buying crappy batteries from the Walgreens down the street that suffice but don't last very long (because you still need batteries in your remote even if they are dinky ones and not the special ones you dreamed lots about). Then one day, five or eight years later, you come home to find this little package on your step. You don't remember ordering anything recently so you are very confused at first and then you bring it inside and open it and there are a ton of these super-special super-deluxe perfect beautiful amazing batteries. It took so long to ship because the people at the battery-packaging plant had to make them first which took a very long time because they are so special then they had to ship them to you in a very meticulous way to make sure they arrived in good condition. Then they felt so bad that it took so long that they threw in, like, twelve more of these batteries into one package to make it up to you. This is a really wonderful surprise because you thought those batteries were never coming and here they are!! And now you will never need another battery ever ever again or at least for a very long time because you have even more than you ordered in the first place! It is like a birthday present from God that you get to be excited about over and over again for the rest of your life. It was like that, if the batteries were all Good Things, and I had ordered them from God in a prayer when I was thirteen, saying, "Please let me fall in love someday," and then God had to take a minute to orchestrate the way I met this person since he lived a very far-away distance from me.

This is when I first discovered that other people can sometimes crank my handle harder than I can. When we would talk, he would idly push my handle around and around and it made my light so bright I could hardly stand it; I wanted to stand up and projectile vomit all over the place because I was so bright and buzzing and Up that I couldn't sit down. That first day we met we sat up until a very early hour in the morning and even though I had to go back to my own hotel room I only slept three hours and woke back up to tell him goodbye, because the way he charged up the lightbulb in my brain felt so good, and since no one had elected to love me before, and since he lived so far away, I assumed he just wanted to be my far-away friend, which was good enough for me. I said goodbye and it felt like saying goodbye to the President or someone else very important and after he got in the car and I could not see him anymore, I looked around at the lobby of the hotel and made a note to remember where everything was. It was very obvious to all parts of my body and spirit that this exact second or minute or year, or however long I was standing there, was a fixed point in time. That no matter what alternate timeline or parallel universe may exist, this moment is one that has happened and will happen in each and every one of them. It felt like God was looking directly at me, like he was watching a movie that he had seen many times before, and even though he knew what was going to happen, he just wanted to see the look on my face when it did. That is a very big thing to be aware of, especially when you are sixteen and running on three hours of sleep.

To my pleasant surprise, things with this man continued after that. Three months into our quaint and friendly affair he revealed to me that on that first day, he was secretly thinking all of the same thoughts I was secretly thinking about how cool things were about each other. We decided that we liked the way we made each other feel so much that we may as well be in love with each other and be done with it! So we were. But being in love is very hard when you're seventeen and eighteen and live two thousand miles apart and have no money to visit each other. It is even harder when one of you is going to college and falling into old habits with the Bad Stuff and the other one is graduating high school and realizing that the sad stuff in their brain is actually quite sick and not going away but is too embarrassed to ask for help. And when all of these things pile up on top of each other, it is very easy to have handles going completely un-cranked for weeks at a time, and it is even easier to become disillusioned with the whole damn thing entirely. Maybe one of you decides being dead sounds like a very good idea and they're going to take it upon themselves to figure that out. Maybe one of you kisses a person who is not the other person in a big whirlwind of confusion. Who's to say? These are just examples.

This man and I, who had once made each other's lights very bright, were no longer generating anything anymore, and as much as being together made it feel like it was going and glowing, the special batteries inside of us had run out of juice. And it was neither of our faults. The batteries were long-lasting and there were a lot of them, but I understood it better as a vacant child: All things die. Unfortunately, now, my heart was filled with empathy and pity and love and a lot of other very heavy things which no longer gave me the option of not-crying or not-feeling-downright-terrible-about-it-all. I became the weak adult I had once despised, but I knew that it was all from good. I would have rather felt the Goodness even for a second than not at all. I know that is cliché but there is a reason it is and it's because it is true.

My wish for him, from the moment I met him, was that one day he would sit down and just start cranking again, and that the momentum would pick up and his arms and hands would be going around and around with that thing, and his light would be so bright that people could see it from Russia and Spain. I loved and admired and envied him so much because I knew that with a generator the size of his, once he started, his light would be damn near the brightest out of everyone in the world. My secret desire was that I would be next to him when it shined again, that I could say, "I knew it all along, even when you people weren't looking!" And he would laugh and say, "Yes, it's true! When nearly all the world turned cold to me, there was one person who knew that I had this inside of me, and I am grateful!" But now because of all the stuff that we had in between us, like love and then not-love and two thousand miles, I know I am fated to be another one of the regular civilians who witnesses his light from afar. But worry not! I will be a very good sport about it and be very happy to see it shining at all, even from a distance, because somewhere inside of my heart his name is carved into a bed frame as my first-ever true love.

My life didn't stop after that. I guess I thought somewhere inside of me that maybe after a big loss like that God or the Universe would be forgiving and at least make stuff slow down for just a second to give me time to get back onto my feet or at least onto my hands and knees because right then I was face-down with my belly on the pavement and my boobs all squished up against my chest and it hurt real bad and felt pretty terrible all around to be honest. And when I feel real terrible like *that* it's like each of my limbs are two hundred pounds and getting up is so out of the question that I'll stay in bed for a whole day without even getting up to eat or pee. Holding in pee is not a very easy thing to do either; after hour eight it starts to hurt in your guts but the hurt doesn't even matter because *that* terrible feeling is much more horrible than any sting from an angry kidney or grumble from a rotting stomach. And, no, life didn't slow down, not even a little bit.

I graduated high school like a Big Guy and summer happened and I don't remember much except I met my first therapist who was a very old lady that was almost too good at listening and not very good at understanding. I took my first medication on and off and decided that going to college was the thing to do because I could no longer shine my light onto anything anymore and people with no lights always either go to college or become a junkie and I was too scared of needles to pick up heroin. So I went to college in Chicago in some sad attempt to get people to get people to be proud of me again since they had also noticed that I wasn't making light anymore and had become less interested in things I had to say. I don't blame them because the stuff I was blabbing about was all pretty much all sad crap about how I didn't feel like anything was how it was supposed to be anymore or whatever. Trying to crank the handle in a time like this was more of a fantasy than a tangible possibility and I started to get scared I wouldn't be able to crank it ever again. This scared me because the light that had previously come out of me was everyone's favorite thing about me; it made me a good and loving person that people wanted to know and talk to and hear things from. Without it? I was no better than the absent-spirited child who did spiteful, selfish things and looked down on others for being comfortable with their humanity! I was empty again. The space inside of me was very dark and thus cold (and I am the type of person who hates winter and loves it when it is eighty degrees outside so you can imagine how much it sucked being inside of me).

When I got to college, I met a new person within about a week of moving into the dorms. Classes hadn't even started yet. I met this one at a very awful party, where no one had any light, where the vodka-lemonades they were serving were more lemonade than anything, where the music they were playing were Top 40's I hadn't heard, and where everyone was dressed the same, all sweaty and pressed up against each other like sardines in this Lincoln Park apartment. I made pouty faces all night with my friend who is actually the king of pouty faces, and went out into the backyard to breathe some clean air that was not heavy-hot-wet-and-thick, and had not been through fifty other pairs of lungs before mine. I had made a note to myself (out loud to my friend) before the party that I had forgotten my cigarettes at the dorm and would have to bum one from someone. My friends helped me scan the crowd. I pointed at him. He was cute and tall and alone and wearing this huge backpack which made me smile for some reason. I trotted up and asked him if I could bum one, and he happily obliged. The way he looked at my face reminded me of how someone else looked at my face once. He asked if I need a lighter and I said no, that I had brought mine, but thank you. Before I zipped away, I told him with a burst of energy from unknown origin that I found him to be very physically attractive, just for his information. I figured I would tell him this nice thing that I thought about him, and he would think, "Weird stranger at a party told me I was pretty: will take this as a compliment," and I would run away and that would be the end of it. But as God would have it, my lighter was nowhere to be found on my person. I was practically *coerced* into returning to him. "Hi," I said, "can I borrow your lighter, actually?" He smirked and pulled out his lighter and then did a very dangerous thing which was saying that corny line about "pretty girls not lighting their own cigarettes" and knowing he was being corny but saying it anyway. The dangerous part about it was calling me pretty because as soon as he said that, some sort of fire started up somewhere inside of me. (I didn't know where yet, and I wouldn't until later - but my first intuition was that he was jiggling my handle around.) We left that party and did the thing I had done with someone before where we stay out until very early in the morning and look at each other with this look in our eyes like we both know a funny secret about the other person but are waiting for the right time to say it. He asked me out at the end of the night and that was that.

Things moved very quickly. I remember an immediate intimacy - within a week it felt like we had been together for three months. We spent nearly every second of every day with each other and most certainly every night. We had a type of physical closeness that was previously unbeknownst to me. It was as if we had known each others bodies since long before this and were just getting reacquainted with all the skin and stuff. Or perhaps in another life the atoms that made up our bodies made up the bodies of two great lovers who were rabbits or Victorian-era secret-partners, or both, and so when those atoms were recycled into ours they met each other again and it was like magnets. I don't know for sure.

The more time I spent around him the more I realized how little we had in common. I did not particularly care for the music he played or the jokes he told or the movies he liked to watch. I did not relate his friends or his stories he told me about who he was from back home in New Jersey. I did not like how his first line of defense was fighting other boys with his fists and how our conversations were rarely stimulating. As much as I hate to admit it, I let more primal matters take reign. I got too involved too quickly to back out when I realized the warmness inside of me was fire of the loins and not love of the heart. Combine that with The New Thing he had shown me and I was caught in an endless crap cycle after the honeymoon phase.

The New Thing was really a Bad Thing disguised as a Good Thing. He showed me how to smoke weed like a big stoner guy and how to be high all the time. The thing I loved most about being high all the time was that all the sad stuff piled up in your brain and heart and hanging off your ribcage like dirty towels and t-shirts from balconies just evaporated. It was like nothing really mattered because your brain turned into a big pillow that was very relaxed and not very worried about finding a job or taking medication every day because all of that was muffled and stifled in the background of your thoughts for an hour or two, and you could still go outside and do things and buy stuff and sometimes it even made doing all of that easier! I remembered what someone who was once my true love told me about how he did too many Bad Things and how he wished I could've met him before he did all of them because he was smarter and faster and brighter and sweeter, and how I always thought it was so sad, because he was still all of these Good Things but the Bad Things made him not know it. But the pillow in my brain muffled that too, and the part about not loving this new boy very much, and the part about not going to any classes means you will fail out of school, because it was just easier not to deal-with-things-and-do-stuff than to deal-with-them-and-do-'em, which is known to be universally true. I started attending parties on weekdays and drinking more. These two things were also great for not thinking about stuff but also felt good inside of me—I found out that if you drink a whole bottle of pink rosé in fifteen minutes, it felt like the generator was moving again, like the light was humming and flashing, and even though it wasn't me pushing the handle around it was someone, reaching a gruesome hand from my stomach or liver to rank that thing, and it felt better than nothing at all. I was duped. I knew I was duped. But being duped is easier than being smart and getting shit done. And without my light I am a coward. So I'm sure you can see how things snowballed into something big and ugly that I did not even want to control.

I went on like that for nine whole months. Yes! Nine months! Nine months of knowing I was very unhappy and wanted out of everything I had gotten myself into. That is the same amount of time that parents spend waiting for babies in tummies and babies are usually the most important thing to ever happen to people! And so all this time that some beautiful cis-het couple probably spent, somewhere out there, maybe on the east coast in a nice Brooklyn apartment, waiting for this new gorgeous toy thing that would actually become the best and loudest pet of all time, I was getting stupider and stupider and knowingly letting it all happen! What a waste!

Then I met someone very important. Well, I didn't meet him just then, I had already met him before, like six or eight months before, but I didn't really *meet* him until that summer after my first-and-only collegiate year. One day he reached out to let me know a fact about something, and I knew (frankly quite instantly) that he was very important and would continue to be so. I don't know who or what tipped me off about this fact but I am willing to bet it was someone like God again. However, it seemed that out of some cruel trick on me, this important person was too many miles away to be seen very easily yet again. So we began doing face-calls and video-chats and saying nice things to each other that were true and showing each other movies and music that was all so very good and wonderful and saying jokes that only we found funny. I am sure you can already guess—his light was so bright that not only was it coming out of his eye holes and nose holes and ear holes and mouth hole but it was even coming out of his *butthole*! He was cranking his own generator and he was cranking mine and I knew I loved him then like a friend's mother who knows you're coming over and has cookies ready every time. He never hesitated to tell me about my little glowing light, still buzzing from the leftover energy of when once I cranked the handle…. *All the while the world turned cold to me, there was one person who saw this inside of me all along! When no one else was looking!* To be on the other side of a sentiment like that was gentle and new to me. No one had been unconditionally kind to me in quite some time, and this unconditional kindness reminded me that I was Good. But I was still deeply involved with all that not-dealing-with-stuff business. So I put off getting better. As long as I could get away with my not-feeling-bad-about-things-I-should-feel-bad-about.

After the year was over and I failed out of all of the classes and had all of the sex and went to all of the parties and met all of the people, my new best friend from college and I took a roadtrip up to where he lived and I got to meet him for the first time in person. It was funny at first but not in a nervous way, and then suddenly it felt like I had had a dream like this a hundred times before and I already knew what was going to happen. Every second spent being his friend was like I was standing in the hotel lobby again; like instead of a fixed point, he was a fixed person. Absolutely unavoidable. He was a very good teacher about showing me how much better everything felt when all the lights were on. That is when I knew for sure. My light had been out for too long and when I returned home, something just had to be done.

The first order of business was saying goodbye to the dinky Walgreens-brand battery I had made a lover and setting him free to be with someone who really loved him and thought the no-good music he made was actually real-good. I did this over the summer and made it official when I saw him again. He was not too happy about not being in control of the breakup so he did many things to be in control of it again. He befriended some of my roommates very closely as a tactical move and came over to my new house/first apartment often to look at me with intense and sad eyes as if to tell me that I should feel very guilty for hurting someone who obviously cares so much about me. Then he said lots of things to me to convince me that I had made some sort of horrific mistake, that our love *was* true and genuine, and that *I* was just *confused*! He added on to all of this by letting me know in underhanded ways that we was sleeping with girls he knew made me insecure (because they were definitely very pretty and good people who didn't have generator issues), doing all of this while still telling me he wanted to be with mc, and lying about it all. I am a very smart person, but being so human as I am, unfortunately, I was emotionally compromised and fell for this evil trick. I made the mistake of opening up a door in my chest for him again. He spared no time finding my generator and smashing it up with his New Jersey fighting fists. He kicked it and spray-painted it with cuss words and hit it with baseball bats. Then he used a screwdriver to unscrew very certain, important screws that he knew were very crucial to holding the whole thing together. When he was done he told me that I made the decision for all of this to happen and I had no one to blame but myself.

After this whole ordeal happened, I had no idea what to do. Most times, I am resourceful or resilient in some way but this time I really had no clue. I looked at all of the pieces of my generator. They were either too badly damaged to be put back together or missing altogether. The handle got buried so deep in my gut that I knew trying to take it out might cause some cuckoo crazy internal bleeding that I just didn't know how to deal with. So I just left it there, and I left all my pieces, scattered and rusting, in my poor fragile body. I assessed all the damage and came to the conclusion that I would not be able to fix it because I was not a mechanic and this thing did not come with any helpful IKEA picture book manual or any manual at all. The one thing that made up all my Good Parts, the one thing that meant anything to me, was all gone, all crushed-up and crumpled and completely pooped-out, and as far as I knew, would never work again. I decided that I would just rather not be an alive person. I decided I would be dead.

Being dead is not as easy as you would think. Being dead takes a lot of time and a lot of effort from the deceased party. To be a dead person you must: turn off your brain, take up as little space as possible, not move, and not speak. You cannot take medications if you are a dead person and you definitely can't eat or pee. But the one thing you super-duper can't do when you're dead is dream. You can't think about if things were worse or if things were better or if things were different at all and you *certainly* can't imagine what the future will be like or even the past. (This was the thing I was least good at while being dead.)

I tried being dead for that whole winter. I slept in my bed for nearly eighteen hours a day, getting up just to eat half a Poptart and then throw it up. I stayed in my bedroom with the blinds closed and I felt myself get really pale and skinny. I was rotting and turning into a skeleton just like a dead person would. I started to smell dead and look dead and I even acted like a ghost, a spirit who had already passed on, moaning about the things I wished I had done while I was alive. My roommates knew I was dead. They all saw me when I would be a ghost in the kitchen or the living room, gracing their presence to score some more Bad Things to make the brain turn off completely. One week I did not eat one single thing. That is how long you can go without eating before you become a real dead thing, you know.

Then something very cool and slightly unforeseen happened. The lovely boy whom I loved very much in a very kind and new but familiar way came to visit me while I was dead. He came to the side of my bed, then a coffin, and looked down at my dead body and kissed my freckled German forehead which reminded me of something I had done once. Then he shook me awake and said, "Look! Look what I did while you were asleep!" And he showed me my new generator. It was all put back together with duct tape and nails and it was working again. I sat up in my tomb with big eyes like a deer or a cousin and said, "How did you do that?" He said, "Easy!" and then sat down next to me in my big terrible chamber and when he did the whole thing turned back into my old white bed and he drew on this big piece of paper some very easy-to-read IKEA instructions for the generator. He said, "Your model is very close to my model, so this is as much as I could figure out; the rest I squished back together.," and for a whole *week* I was in awe of this feat. We went out to eat and I put lots of food in my mouth and it all tasted good. I drank a lot of water and peed it all out when I had to and remembered to take my dainty little medications. I talked and laughed so much and so loud I thought my head was going to fall off. My brain was on and it was fast like the operating systems had been updated and the viruses had been attacked by some holy malware protection. That week I took up a lot of space in the world. That week I was really big.

All of these things you cannot do as a dead person. He made me alive again while he was there. All this gratefulness for his companionship to me, even when I was not my best, welled up in my stomach and it hasn't stopped being there ever since. But sometimes a big feeling like gratefulness or admiration can take a shape that looks a lot like love!

Love is a very tricky thing to pin down and I think I got very lucky once before. Growing up and seeing my parents be very in love and say things like, "Marry your best friend," and, "When we got married we became one person," while also being acutely aware of the rarity of monogamy and that 50% of marriages end in divorce snowballed into an acute fear of never finding a lifelong partner and thus never feeling whole.

So here it is: the part about the freezing. I hope you are not too mad that I took up all this time telling you about loves and not-loves and batteries and dangerous things to say at parties. And I hope you were not too bored or saddened with the part about the Bad Things disguised as Good Things that I was so totally warned about or the smashing of special things by ill-intentioned not-very-smart people, who I was also warned about. But we are here.

A few months went by after my reanimation and the next summer I moved into a new house. More months went by and then some more months and more and a few more. Things appeared sweet and fine. I hadn't even realized I had frozen myself! Yes that's right! I did the freezing *without even noticing*! I bet you'd think that a big process like that would be pretty noticeable, but you're wrong. As soon as the lovely boy who I loved all brand-new left my house that mid-cruelwinter I started the freezing process. Someone in charge upstairs made up their mind that I was stuck in-between bad and better and that I was just supposed to wait until things got to the better half. They also decided that I was in love with this kind boy and that *only he* would ever be able to make my generator work again. I figured if I waited long enough, things would shake out, and his love for me would grow as mine did, in the same direction, like plants tied to skewers with yarn bows to make sure they go up and don't break or topple over.

But what I had done was cryogenically freeze myself. I was still alive in there, but I didn't know it. My skin was frozen and I felt pleasant because when you're frozen you don't feel much emotion rather than just *content* or *pleasant* or that you've done *just enough* and *can't do much more than this* which would technically qualify as doing your best. Because I was alive and not dead this time, I thought, "I am doing well! I am doing better!" But the truth of the matter was that I hadn't done anything differently at all. I was waiting, maybe for a month, maybe for five hundred years, for something good to happen to me. Something big and good enough to get me back on my own crank. I convinced myself I was trying, improving, but I was doing so literally nothing different at all that some days the scientists who monitored my cryogenic chamber would get an alert on their computers telling them I was dead in there, and they would all get up in a panic and rush over and open the thing and check my vitals, and my heart would still be beating and my brain would still be dreaming, and they would think, "At least they're still alive," and go back to drinking coffee and playing darts or whatever it is scientists do when their job is monitoring frozen people.

And then to be thawed.

Somewhere in my frozen state, I became very aware that waiting and being frozen was not doing much help and got very desperate and sad because the whole reason I had frozen myself in the first place was because I thought waiting it out would yield some divine intervention. But the difference between being dead and frozen is that when you are frozen you can still think a lot about stuff, and dream. Being frozen is very similar to being empty in that it is cold and not very polite-feeling. It dawned on me in this half-alive homeostasis that waiting for things really does not work the way I thought it did and that if I want Good Things I have to go get them. But when you're frozen it is very hard to move, so hard that it seems almost pathetic to even try. Additionally, I am a terribly, awfully, horribly stubborn creature. There is no way around that. So I said, *Fine. I will take my frozen body to the boy that I love who does not love me and if he cannot start my engine again then I will just have to put some sort of end to all this because it has been going on for far too long and I am very tired and I'm very tired of being very tired. Plus, I have test-run being dead once before and I think I can do it for real and forever this time. That is easier than doing the other thing which would be to force myself to start caring and doing which happens to be a lot of work, as I'm sure you're well aware.*

So I went to visit the boy in the west who I thought I loved but didn't really and as soon as the plane landed I got this weird gooey feeling in my arms like I get when I am wrong about something. As soon as I saw him again I knew it. It had been a long time since that winter of my assisted resurrection and it was clear so much had changed that I didn't even notice because I was too busy fantasizing in my frozen state.

Then I met his new girlfriend. She was beautiful, adorned with a genuinely kind heart, and a lovely generator she cranked all by herself. I realized it was very silly of me to want to love anyone right now when I was still so cold to the touch. She was so wonderful and pure and I understood they provided something for each other that I was still unable yet to provide for myself. It made perfect sense then, and only hurt a little bit because it felt silly of me to have let Admiration and Gratitude trick me into thinking they were someone as famous and as popular as Love!

On Friday night, the boy and I got into a big fight, mostly fueled by my own frustration with myself that I was stuck with all these realizations and was having so much trouble being lit-up anymore, and that I knew it made it very hard for him to be my friend. He had to go somewhere in a hurry so I cried like a child and he saw all that, then he left and I just sat in his apartment which happened to be too quiet at this particular moment. I didn't know what else to do and so, in a fit of rage, I chucked my heart (still frozen) at the floor. And when frozen things get chucked at stuff they almost always shatter, which is exactly what happened to my heart. It became a bunch of tiny cold pieces that were very sharp like shards of glass and these shards went all over the floor in this boy's apartment. I tried to pick them up because I felt bad about making such a mess but then these pieces pierced my hands and got stuck in my skin like thorns and sticky thistles except these hurt much more. I knew right then that I had to be dead at the soonest possible moment because there was absolutely no way that all of this Big Bad Feeling would ever go away because it was just too big and just too bad and no one in the history of feelings had ever felt something of this magnitude and lived. Then something different happened.

The boy must've left a window open or something, because all the hot heat and wind from the fires burning Los Angeles down got right up into my nose and mouth and I breathed it in and just thawed right there. All the layers of ice on my skin melted off and surrounded me with a little pool of water that my tears blended perfectly into, and the shards of my heart became gelatin and fell right out of my hands. I was ten thousand pounds lighter without all of that ice and looked down at the big puddle that had been Me for several months, or perhaps a few years, and I saw my face in the reflection. My hair looked longer than I remembered and my eyebrows were bleached white and my cheeks were scarred and pink. The thing about being alive *and* unfrozen is that you can open your eyes and see what things really look like right in front of you instead of just imagining what you think *should* or *might* be there. The first thing I did was call my mom.

It felt instinctual. It was. When I was seven, I had surgery to remove my obscenely oversized tonsils. Before I went under, they told me several times, "When you wake up, it is important that you do not yell. Your throat will be very sore and it will hurt." I said okay and they gave me the bubblegum gas that made me sleep deeply. When the whole thing was over-with and I came to in the hospital bed, I wasted no time letting out a raspy yet impressively bloodcurdling scream for my mother. This was the same.

On the phone she told me lots of things that she always tells me, but this time they made logical sense to me. They had never done that before all the other time she had said those things to me and it was like suddenly understanding a whole new language. It was my first time in the entirety of the twenty years I'd been walking the planet that I asked for help and meant it. Without shame, too, which had been a problem in the past. This was a different feeling but not different-bad; definitely different-good like when you're sitting in precalculus and suddenly you know why you're using that equation for that problem and it all falls into place. We made plans for when I got back to make some appointments and get me back on my feet. Then I said thank you and goodbye and I love you, and all the other things you say to your mother on the phone when you thought you were about to die but you didn't.

I sat on the boy's tiny couch and for the first time in a very long time felt light like helium, like if I wasn't wearing my heavy loafers that I would just up and bounce around on the ceiling. I smiled because I was happy and I was happy and I was happy. I had done a Good Thing just then, and a very important thing, and maybe God wasn't looking right at me but he was definitely giving me a side-eye at the very least. I put on a jacket and went outside and wandered around the neighborhood and I laughed and I laughed so hard that I cried because I had been an ant under a big mean toddler's shoe for twenty years and finally I got powerful enough to push the shoe off. A big mean toddler who offered ignorance for experience and I declined. And I sang and danced in the street because I didn't care again, because somehow I managed even now to get myself down there and start cranking my handle even if it was slow, even if my muscles were not strong enough, because I had wasted enough time being dead and frozen that now I had a lot of life to catch up on. Suddenly all this new knowledge just appeared in my brain and it went like this: if I want Big Things I have to *go get small things* first. And if I don't kick my own ass into cranking my own stupid broken-but-fixed generator handle again no one ever would and that's not scary or sad that's just the fact of the matter.

"And another thing," The Universe said silently by waving its little (great big) finger at me. I was reminded then that if my head gets too big it can more easily get knocked off my shoulders. I nodded, and a big, clean wind of forgiveness swept through me and everyone who I held in a tiny wet fist of resentment just vanished. I looked them all in the faces and said, "It was not about you it was about me! and I know that is the worst breakup line in history but I need you to know I understand now!" I said goodbye to those parts, and then some other parts of me that had previously been discouragement turned into inspiration.

I sang to God and said, "Thank you very much for showing me all of these things," then called the boy and told him in some other words that I was sorry for throwing such a big fit in his house and that I knew I wasn't even a whole-alive person and I was *glad* that this was the situation because whole people deserve to love other whole people, and I needed to see him all whole to recognize all the parts I was still missing. I apologized to him for putting all that pressure on him because it really was not fair. He said thank you for understanding and we went on being good friends and when he came home later that night our lights were both on, next to each other, really dim and slowly cranked because we were very tired from all the feeling, but still glowing and humming minutely. And I was proud of myself then, for being ready to be alive, and for wanting to be.

Some deep-down voice in me told me then that a Great Role had been played in my life and that because of all the commotion and drama I caused in his studio apartment in the middle of burning-down Los Angeles, that our friendship with each other would not ever be like it was and part of me mourned that and another part rejoiced because I knew, with all the rest of my brand new knowings, that my expectations were for two different people who were simply not us anymore. I became an adult right there on his couch and in the corner of his kitchen where the puddle was and maybe one day I would tell him that and maybe I wouldn't.

On the plane ride home, my freshly thawed brain, though feeling a bit soggy, was mumbling with electricity and I heard rumors spinning and ricocheting around my dome like, "The Bitch is Back!"

and, "The Evil has Been Defeated!" I am still not sure exactly what the implications of those revelations are supposed to be, but I can tell, surely and truly, that whatever body came out of that cryogenic freezing was a different one, a bigger one, and an older one. I thought to myself then that this must be what a butterfly feels like! when it is all done with its cocoon, all done with its waiting to be whole and beautiful and free, and that much like a butterfly I was going to go after my sweet things and pretty things.

Later I would pass a mother and child on the moving walkway in the airport. The child was absolutely no taller than four feet (and if he was, he is free to file a libel lawsuit against me when he turns eighteen because I would like to be held accountable if ever defacing the reputation of an airport child's height). I imagined what I looked like in his eyes, and somehow I knew, to him, I was an adult, in the same way I saw my older cousins at Christmases and Thanksgivings when I was four and five and ten. Children are very good at seeing things as they plainly are, and it comforted me to know that plainly, I had metamorphosed. But I kept my head about me and reminded myself that I still had a lot of metamorpho-sizing left to do if I wanted to keep these new wings and these defrosted, living body parts, and that it was not going to be easy to crank the generator any time soon. But the deal was that I just had to do it because if I did, eventually it would become easier to do it than to not-do it, like when I was a child who had just canoodled a corpse, which is really my dream of all dreams.

And so I would.

That is the story of how I died and came back, was frozen and unfrozen, was loved and not loved, was empty then full then empty then full again, and how after all that, I turned out to be alive and not dead, and generally okay with it all, even though I thought I wouldn't be.

HUGO GERNSBACK

1939

SAM MOSKOWITZ

WILL S. SYKORA

JAMES V. TAURASI

JOHN TAINE

FORREST J ACKERMAN

MOROJO (MYRTLE DOUGLAS)

JACK DARROW

JULIUS SCHWARTZ

MARIO RACIC JR.

Thank You.
Thank You.
THANK YOU.
Thank You.
Thank You.
Thank You.
Thank You.
THANK YOU.
Thank You.

Chloe Frances Woodard

Made in the USA
Monee, IL
06 June 2020

32681184R00076